KEVIN SPACEY'S ABORTED TRIAL

Michael Wells Glueck

Author, *Living Among The Swiss*
The Trial of Thomas E. Toolan III
Neil Entwistle's Day In Court
The Retirement Home Experience
What I Learned At University
The Nantucket Rape Trial
Two 2017 Nantucket Rape Trials

Kevin Spacey's Aborted Trial

Copyright © 2019: Michael Wells Glueck
All rights reserved

ISBN-10: 1-081-36826-8
ISBN-13: 978-1-081-36826-5

No part of this book may be reproduced in any form or by any means, graphic, electronic, or mechanical, including photocopying, recording, taping, or by any information storage or retreval systems, without written permission from the publisher.

Published by: EditAndPublishYourBook.com
Proprietor: Michael Wells Glueck
E-Mail: MichaelTheAuthor@Gmail.com

As a criminal trial buff, I attended from the arraignment the court hearings pertaining to Kevin Spacey's alleged assault of an eighteen-year-old busboy at a bar in Nantucket, Massachusetts on July 7, 2016. That event was amply covered by the popular press, both in and out of the courtroom. Seated there half an hour before proceedings began, I was interviewed by a female reporter from the *New York Post* and by a male reporter from the *Boston Herald*.

To both, I stated my belief that the charge was exaggerated. Mr.

Spacey, under his legal name of Kevin Fowler, was charged with plying the off-duty busboy with drinks at a local upscale bar, unzipping the lad's fly, inserting both hands, and massaging the genitals over the underwear. Having tried this with several pairs of my own trousers on pants hangers, I demonstrated to my own satisfaction that it is not possible for an adult with normally sized hands to insert more than one at a time into an open fly. The victim's mother, who in 2017 had told NBC's Kate Snow that the actor had "put his hand in" her son's fly, made the two-handed claim in television interviews after the arraignment was announced, but, at a subsequent court appearance reduced that charge back to a single intrusive hand.

 The judge admonished the actor to avoid being charged with another offense "while this matter is pending," lest he subject himself to being held without bail for ninety days by the Commonwealth, and to avoid contacting the alleged victim by any means. Mr. Spacey nodded wearily at the latter instruction.

At two subsequent hearings, the defendant's lead attorney, Alan Jackson, pressed District Court Judge Thomas Barrett, a self-described "Quincy boy," for an early trial date in the summer of 2019. The first time, the judge explained that jury trials in Nantucket are held only once every two months, and that his crowded docket meant that "That won't happen." The likeliest trial date, he said, would be some time in November. Mr. Spacey attended the next hearing, and for his benefit the request was repeated. In his amplified response, the judge added that the courtroom also served as the venue for Superior Court, Juvenile Court, and the Land Court; that because of the publicity attending the case it would be necessary to interview an unusually large number of prospective jurors; and that it would be unfair to move this case ahead of many other defendants awaiting trial, some of them currently in custody. He added that in summer the lawyer might find that "accommodations are tight."

    At both of these hearings, the defense team included

attorney Jim Lawson, who four years earlier had successfully defended J. Michael Robison against a spurious charge of having raped his female interior decorator – a woman with whom, he was later reported to have told a contracted workman, he had been having an affair for the previous two years. I had published a book about this matter, *The Nantucket Rape Trial*, and during the trial I had made the acquaintance of Mr. Lawson, who greeted me warmly at the Spacey hearing, said he remembered me and had enjoyed reading my book.

Two pretrial hearings later, after the alleged victim and his parents reported being unable to find a cell phone with which the former busboy had recorded the encounter, Mr. Lawson was absent, conceivably signifying that the defense already expected the case to be dismissed before trial, and that Mr. Lawson's intended role had been to interrogate some witnesses and to deliver the closing argument.

A week before the next hearing, the accuser filed and two days later withdrew a civil suit against Mr. Spacey in

Nantucket Superior Court seeking unspecified damages for his alleged emotional distress, inability to work, and consequent lost earnings actual and potential. This suit was dismissed without prejudice, so that it can be reinstated at the plaintiff's discretion. He indicated that he prefers to deal with only one such matter at a time. His mother subsequently denied that the civil case was withdrawn because an out-of-court settlement had been reached.

At the dramatic hearing on July 8, 2019, I had the pleasure

of sitting next to and conversing with Louisa Moller, a lovely, friendly, and well informed reporter for WBZ, the Boston CBS affiliate. We, along with others in the courtroom, watched the accuser admit deleting some items from the missing phone, but then take the Fifth after being advised by Attorney Jackson that Massachusetts law makes it a felony to delete relevant information pursuant to a criminal investigation or trial, he took the Fifth.

Then his mother, a former WCVB news anchor named

Heather Unruh ("balance" or, literally, "unrest" in German), after laughingly admitting that she had consumed alcohol in the past twenty-four hours though not that morning, waived her own Fifth Amendment right against self-incrimination – "I was raised to tell the truth" – also admitted deleting "a few irrelevant" items ("frat boy activities") from the phone. Mr. Jackson admonished her that "you don't get to decide what is relevant: I do, the prosecution does, and, ultimately, the judge does." The witness then admitted that her son "like all twenty year-olds" had used marijuana and had "possessed a fake ID" to enable him to buy and be served alcohol. She was vague about the whereabouts of the phone, claiming that the events in question had happened "a long time ago." She then tried futilely to shift the focus away from the missing cell phone and back to the alleged assault, for which, however, no witness has come forward, no evidence adduced. Judge Barrett twice instructed her to limit her responses to the questions posed by Attorney Jackson. She vehemently denied referring to the alleged assailant as a "faggot," affirming that "I never use that word." When she claimed that no one wished the phone to be found more than she, Mr. Jackson retorted, "I beg to differ." And when she predicted a conviction if a related video on the missing phone were recovered, he snapped back, "We'll see." Given the same warning about Massachusetts law as that provided to her son, she said she was "beginning to understand" her vulnerable legal position.

    A state trooper testified that he had returned the cell phone to the accuser's father, and both he and a colleague admitted that he had not observed the usual procedure of requesting a receipt. Subsequently, the Cape and Islands district attorney's office announced that it had instituted a rule requiring receipts in such instances.

Then the accuser's father took the stand, claimed that he had "no recollection" of having received the phone from the trooper, and proved even more combative than his wife. As he had done with the mother, the judge twice admonished him to limit his responses to the questions asked. And when, in response to one question, he erupted, "I think you ask too many questions that have nothing to do with this case," the judge -- with a courtroom guard hovering near the witness stand -- warned him that he was in imminent danger of being cited for contempt, adding at one point, "You're real close."

"I understand," the witness replied.

"Thank you," answered the judge.

A bench conference ensued, during which the defense demanded immediate dismissal of the case against Mr. Spacey. Seeming to agree partially, Judge Barrett replied that a dismissal might indeed be in the offing, and he requested such a motion from the defense team plus a response from prosecutor Brian Glenny.

Incidentally, Mr. Glenny successfully prosecuted Thomas E. Toolan III for the murder of Elizabeth Lochtefeld in 2007 in Nantucket and, after the Supreme Judicial Court ordered a new trial in 2011, at the retrial in Barnstable. The second jury took only three hours to find the defendant guilty once more, two-thirds of the time spent deliberating by the first jury in Nantucket. Please see my account of the first proceeding, *The Trial of Thomas E. Toolan III*.

The next pretrial hearing was provisionally scheduled for July 31 in Nantucket. If the accuser persists in taking the Fifth, Judge Barrett will probably dismiss the case. Ironically, at a previous hearing, Mr. Glenny had facetiously suggested that Mr. Jackson file a motion for dismissal! This was before the accuser's cell phone -- an iPhone 5 -- was reported as missing, and when the defense was hoping to retrieve its metadata – which, however, are not impervious to deletion.

After each hearing, regardless of whether the actor had been in attendance, paparazzi clustered outside the main entrance of the Town and Country building to snap photos and to shout questions at Attorney Jackson, who ignored them and forged resolutely ahead.

On July 17, the Cape and Islands District Attorney's office announced that the sexual assault and battery charge against Mr. Spacey had been dropped. Three days earlier – a Sunday – according to the press release, a meeting of the young accuser and his parents had been held in the D.A.'s office, at which the alleged victim, who had been warned that the case would be dismissed if he persisted in asserting his Fifth Amendment right against self-incrimination, stated that after private reflection he had decided not to waive that right.

 The questions remain: where is the cell phone, and what could it reveal about the alleged incident. Theoretically, the alleged victim and his parents could be the subjects of further investigations by state police. But I suspect that authorities will not pursue the matter.

In other jurisdictions – London and Los Angeles – there are ongoing investigations of Mr. Spacey's alleged conduct with other accusers who have made numerous complaints. Again according to NBC's Kate Snow, authorities in Los Angeles have promised that a decision as to whether to prosecute will be forthcoming "soon."

But at least for the moment Mr. Spacey, while not indicated, is off the hook, as he predicted in a video, released just after he was initially carged, in which he assumed his role as Frank Underwood in "House of Cards": "If I've gotten away with things I did do, you don't think I'll pay for something I didn't do, now, do you?" And he asked his fans not to rush to judgment: "I know what you want: You want me back. You wouldn't rush to judgment without facts, would you?"

I do think the Massachusetts case should have been dismissed. Although available cell phone records do show the alleged victim calling for help at least once, he reportedly endured the claimed groping for approximately three minutes, until the actor abruptly left for the restroom. During that interval, the star-struck youth apparently made no effort to remove the hand inside his trousers, instead taking videos of what was happening and sending them to his skeptical girlfriend in order to convince her that he really was experiencing an encounter with Kevin Spacey. (The video, a state trooper admitted to Attorney Jackson, showed only the actor touching the alleged victim's shoulder.) Moreover, he waited seventeen months to report the incident to police.

    Moreover, in my limited experience, casual touching at bars is not uncommon. One evening in the 1970s, when I went to Friday's on First Avenue at Sixty-Third Street in Manhattan to dance and to socialize, an inebriated young woman approached me and asked, "Are you blond?"

Pointing to my hair, I replied, "You can see that I am." "No," she explained, "I mean down there." And without encouragement she reached for my zipper pull but was stopped by her boyfriend. In 2000, at another high-class bar in Nantucket, I saw a chap raise his girlfriend's skirt to display her legs. (I smiled, and she smiled back flirtatiously, but I rejected the bait.) In neither case did any observer object or act as though something unusual had occurred.

www.ingramcontent.com/pod-product-compliance
Lightning Source LLC
Chambersburg PA
CBHW021858170526
45157CB00006B/2510